Making Movies in Technicolor

Lisa Holewa

✳ Smithsonian

Contributing Author

Heather Schultz, M.A.

Consultants

Joyce Bedi
*Head of Ed., Lemelson Center for
the Study of Invention & Innovation
National Museum of American History*

Tamieka Grizzle, Ed.D.
*K–5 STEM Lab Instructor
Harmony Leland Elementary School*

Stephanie Anastasopoulos, M.Ed.
*TOSA, STREAM Integration
Solana Beach School District*

Publishing Credits

Rachelle Cracchiolo, M.S.Ed., *Publisher*

Conni Medina, M.A.Ed., *Managing Editor*

Diana Kenney, M.A.Ed., NBCT, *Series Developer*

Véronique Bos, *Creative Director*

Robin Erickson, *Art Director*

June Kikuchi, *Content Director*

Seth Rogers, *Editor*

Mindy Duits, *Senior Graphic Designer*

Smithsonian Science Education Center

Image Credits: front cover, p.1, p.14 (all) AF archive/Alamy; back cover PacificCoastNews/Newscom; p.4 (left), p.8 (top) Public Domain via Wikimedia; p.4 (right), p.7 M.G.M/Album/Newscom; p.5 (top) Chadwick Pictures/Ronald Grant Archive/Alamy; p.6 (left) Marcin Wichary/Creative Commons via Wikimedia; p.8 (bottom) BSIP/Science Source; p.9 public Domain/Wikimedia; p.10 Timothy J. Bradley; p.11 Kevin Panter; p.12, p.19, p.25 (bottom) RGR Collection/Alamy; p.13 Adam Hart-Davis/Science Source; p.15 Roger L. Wollenberg/UPI/Newscom; p.16 (left) SSPL/Getty Images; p.16 (right) Bettmann/Getty Images; p.17 (insert) Library of Congress [LC-USZ62-115734]; p.18 (left) SilverScreen/Alamy; p.18 (right) Moviestore collection Ltd/Alamy; p.20 Entertainment Pictures/Alamy; p.20 (bottom) Everett Collection; p.21, p.24 Pictorial Press Ltd/Alamy; p.22 (left) H. Armstrong Roberts/ClassicStock/Science Source; p.23 Keystone Pictures USA/Alamy; p.25 (top) Buena Vista Pictures/Everett Collection; pp.26–27 World History Archive/Newscom; all other images from iStock and/or Shutterstock.

Library of Congress Cataloging-in-Publication Data

Names: Holewa, Lisa, author.
Title: Making movies in Technicolor / Lisa Holewa.
Description: Huntington Beach, CA : Teacher Created Materials, [2019] | Includes index. |
Identifiers: LCCN 2018005246 (print) | LCCN 2018016605 (ebook) | ISBN 9781493869381 (E-book) | ISBN 9781493866984 (pbk.)
Subjects: LCSH: Color cinematography--History--Juvenile literature. | Color motion pictures--History--Juvenile literature. | Technicolor, Inc.--History--Juvenile literature.
Classification: LCC TR853 (ebook) | LCC TR853 .H65 2019 (print) | DDC 777--dc23
LC record available at https://lccn.loc.gov/2018005246

Smithsonian

Teacher Created Materials

5301 Oceanus Drive
Huntington Beach, CA 92649-1030
www.tcmpub.com
ISBN 978-1-4938-6698-4
©2019 Teacher Created Materials, Inc.

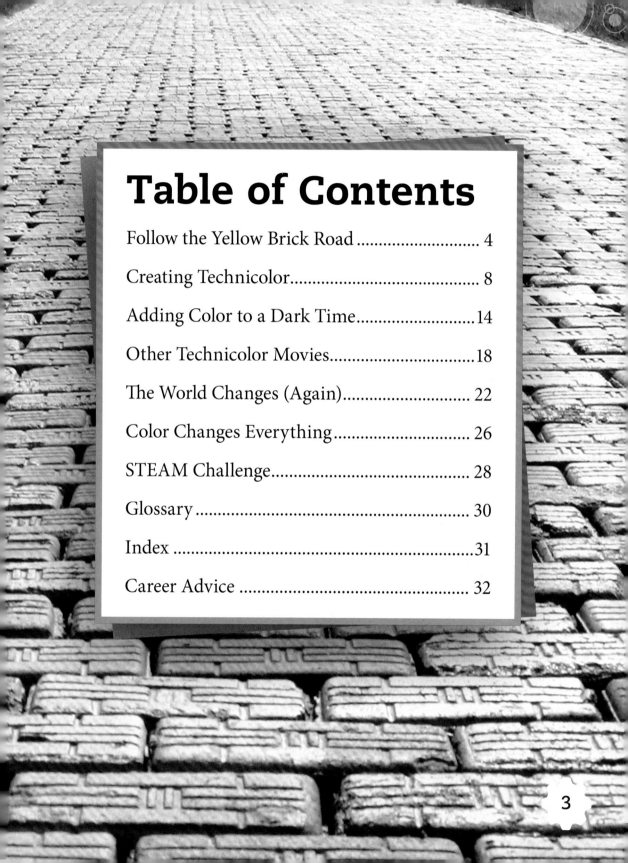

Table of Contents

Follow the Yellow Brick Road

Have you heard of the yellow brick road? What about Dorothy's ruby slippers? You might recognize them from the movie *The Wizard of Oz*. But why do people still connect them to a film that came out more than 75 years ago?

One answer is the colors. The red slippers and yellow brick road are memorable because they were so **vibrant**. The same can be said for the film's sparkling Emerald City and the bright-green Wicked Witch of the West.

The Story of Oz

The Wizard of Oz film is based on a children's book written by L. Frank Baum. It tells the story of a girl named Dorothy. She lives on a farm in Kansas with her aunt and uncle. When a tornado hits, she and her dog, Toto, are carried away to the Land of Oz.

The Wonderful Wizard of Oz book was first published in 1900. It quickly became a best seller. Within two years, it was made into a play. The play was made into a short film in 1910. It was then made into a full-length movie in 1925.

The Wizard of Oz
1925 film poster

The 1925 film version of *The Wizard of Oz* does not include Dorothy's dog, Toto. There is also no Wicked Witch and no yellow brick road!

Back then, movies did not have sound. Those movies are called silent films. They were usually shown while live musicians played in the theaters. Music helped set the mood of the movies. Stories were told mostly through actors' actions and facial expressions. Black screens with text and dialogue also helped explain stories. By the early 1930s, movies with sound (called talkies) took over.

In 1939, the Oz movie most people today know and love was made. This version starred Judy Garland. Not only did it have sound, but it also showed the scenes of Oz in full color.

From Black and White to Technicolor

Today, anyone can film full-color videos using a smartphone. But when movies first came out, they were all black and white. The ability to **transfer** color to film didn't exist yet. That changed thanks to a process called Technicolor.

three-strip Technicolor movie camera

The Wizard of Oz was not the first movie to use color. When it came out, it wasn't a major hit. But it used color in a way that makes it hard to imagine the film without it. Without a doubt, color made the movie better.

In the children's book *The Wonderful Wizard of Oz*, Dorothy's slippers are not red. They are sparkly silver!

Judy Garland as Dorothy Gale

Creating Technicolor

The process used for *The Wizard of Oz* is called Technicolor. Herbert Kalmus, Daniel Frost Comstock, and W. Burton Wescott created the first Technicolor process in 1915. It made movies colorful. But the process did not really film the movies in color. That would not be possible for several more **decades**. Instead, it used special cameras to record films through **filters**.

This frame of film used the first Technicolor process.

How Do Eyes Perceive Color?

Eyes and brains work together to see color. Light moves in long and short waves. When light hits an object, the waves bounce off and hit parts of the eye called rod cells and cone cells. These rods and cones react to the different light waves and send messages to the brain. The brain decodes these messages as color.

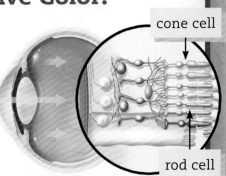

cone cell

rod cell

From Two Filters to Three

In Technicolor's first process, light passed through the lens of a camera and into a prism. In the middle of the prism was a mirror that split the light in two directions. Each camera had two colored filters. One was red and the other green. The film frames were shown together, creating color images.

But there were problems. The movies had to be played through a special projector. It was hard to match the pictures perfectly. And certain colors didn't work. Green and red could not be mixed to create good blues or bright yellows. Skies sometimes looked green. Purple could come out looking black or brown. This made Technicolor hard for filmmakers to use and hard for film watchers to enjoy.

This frame of film used the second Technicolor process.

Perfecting Technicolor took a few tries. The Technicolor company worked hard to make colors on film look more realistic. One way people improved the process was by adding a blue color filter. Now, there were three filters. They also learned how to **dye** colors directly onto the film. By the time *The Wizard of Oz* was made, they had mastered this color **technique**. It was called Technicolor Process 4.

Process 4 used cameras that recorded on three strips of film at a time instead of one strip. Light still passed through the camera lens and into a prism. This split the light in two directions. As it left the prism, light passed through colored filters. Half of the light passed through a green filter onto one filmstrip. The other half passed through a **magenta** filter, which recorded blue on one filmstrip and red on another. The filmstrips were printed on gels. Then, the gels were dyed, and the color was carefully layered onto a blank piece of film.

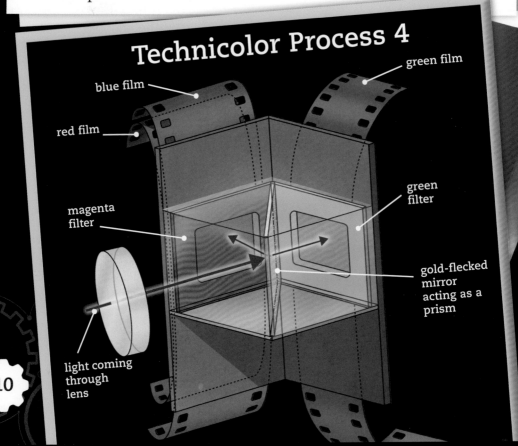

Technicolor Process 4

blue film

green film

red film

green filter

magenta filter

gold-flecked mirror acting as a prism

light coming through lens

Different Layers in the Technicolor Process

Cameras record negatives on three strips of film.

Red Green Blue

Images are printed on filmstrips.

Red Green Blue

Filmstrips are dyed.

Cyan Magenta Yellow

Colors are layered onto new film to make it colorized.

Critics of Color

Not everyone believed adding color to films was worth it. Some movie lovers worried that adding color would ruin films. They feared that people would just like the newness of color. They thought the story and imagination of movies would be lost.

These critics of color thought it was just a gimmick. Part of the problem was that the early two-color process didn't work that well. The odd colors sometimes made the movie worse instead of better.

Color as Art

One of the films that first changed people's minds about color was called *The Black Pirate*. It came out in 1926 and starred Douglas Fairbanks. It used that earlier two-color process. But Fairbanks knew it was important to control how each color looked. So he had a ship and an entire set built in his studio. Even the palm trees were made. Leaves were painted on the trees so they would be the perfect color. The movie wasn't just colorful. It was artistic. The color made the movie better. His success helped other filmmakers decide to use color.

DOUGLAS FAIRBANKS in The BLACK PIRATE

zoetrope

TECHNOLOGY

First Motion Picture

Horse in Motion is an example of an early moving image. It is really just photos of a horse running. The movie used the same technology as a popular children's toy called a zoetrope (ZOH-ee-trohp). The toy makes pictures look like they are moving by spinning them quickly past viewing slits. It's like a flip-book, except pictures are seen through slits in a circular container.

Adding Color to a Dark Time

There had been several popular color movies by the time *The Wizard of Oz* was made. The new Technicolor process had been improved. It made color look good on film.

But those weren't the only reasons color worked so well in *The Wizard of Oz*. There was another reason why color made the film better. The movie came out during the Great Depression. Life was **bleak**. People went to the movies to escape the sadness of life.

The Wizard of Oz was magical. One of the most magical parts was the color. The movie opens in a sort of black-and-white shade called sepia (SEE-pee-uh). These scenes look grim, like real life did. Then, Dorothy opens the door to Oz. Everything bursts forth in beautiful Technicolor!

In the movie, Oz was a special place. The rich colors made the movie special, too. Color wasn't being used as a gimmick. It was an important way to tell the story.

Technicolor

sepia

One Technicolor camera with its gear weighed 181 kilograms (400 pounds)! One is currently on display at Smithsonian's National Museum of American History in Washington, DC.

Bright Lights and Loud Noises

The Wizard of Oz was made using eight special cameras that each recorded on three strips of film. Each camera had trained people operating it. There was a lot of other extra equipment, too. The set was very crowded.

For the cameras to work, the set needed to be well lit. This meant using very bright lights. Some actors said the lights damaged their eyes. The lights also gave off a lot of heat. The set was often over 38° Celsius (100° Fahrenheit). Actors wore heavy costumes. So, they needed to drink a lot of water so they wouldn't pass out.

The cameras were also very loud. Engineers had to add covers over them to **muffle** the noise. Without doing so, it would have been hard to hear what the actors were saying.

Covers made the cameras even bigger. Making *The Wizard of Oz* was not easy. Everyone had to work together to make sure the film came out right.

view inside a three-color camera

A Technicolor camera is set up to film a scene for a movie.

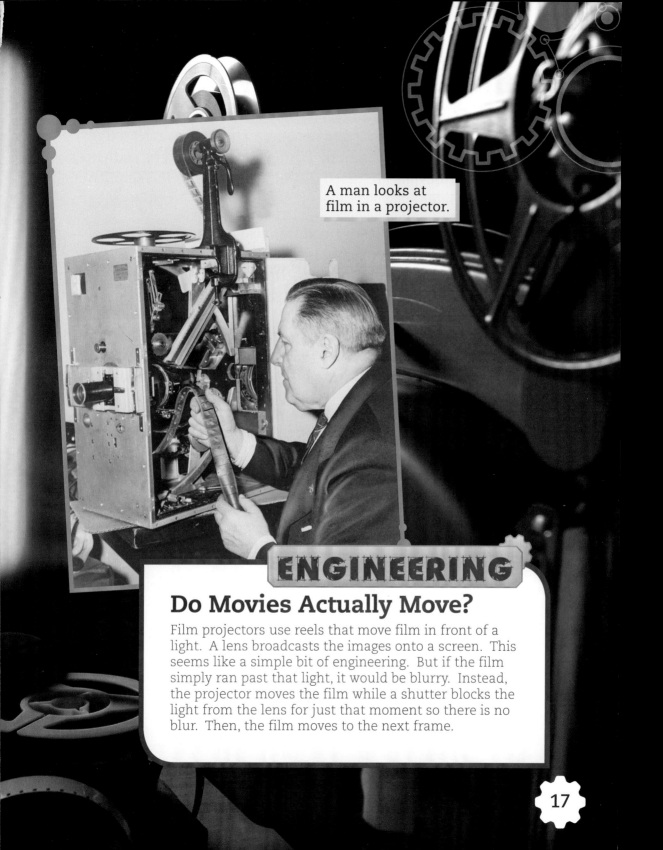

A man looks at film in a projector.

ENGINEERING

Do Movies Actually Move?

Film projectors use reels that move film in front of a light. A lens broadcasts the images onto a screen. This seems like a simple bit of engineering. But if the film simply ran past that light, it would be blurry. Instead, the projector moves the film while a shutter blocks the light from the lens for just that moment so there is no blur. Then, the film moves to the next frame.

Other Technicolor Movies

Besides *The Wizard of Oz*, there were many films that used Technicolor. *Snow White and the Seven Dwarfs* was released in 1937. It is a Walt Disney film. Disney loved color. His audiences did, too. Disney also released the hit film *Fantasia* in Technicolor a few years later.

The Adventures of Robin Hood was also a huge production. It used all 11 Technicolor cameras that existed at the time. The movie had to show vibrant colors. Robin Hood wore green. The noblemen wore rich colors, such as red. The differences between them had to be clear.

Gone with the Wind was another important movie. It was the first color film to win an Oscar for Best Picture. The movie cost more to make than almost any other film at the time.

Why did Technicolor become so popular? The new process made colors look better. Filmmakers understood how to use it well. They used color to tell their stories. Moviegoers loved seeing stories told in color.

The Adventures of Robin Hood

Natalie Kalmus

ARTS

Making It All Look Good Together

Making Technicolor films was a complicated art form. Studios hired cameramen and color consultants from Technicolor to make sure things looked beautiful on film. Natalie Kalmus is the artist to thank the most for this process. She made all decisions about color when Technicolor movies were filmed. She decided on costumes and makeup. She made sure sets had balanced colors. She oversaw lighting. She did all this and more to make sure colors looked vibrant and rich on-screen.

Color, Music, and Dance

In the 1950s, people were in love with musicals. Many of them were filmed in Technicolor.

A very popular musical of the time was *Singin' in the Rain*. It is about a movie star who falls in love with a chorus girl. Movie fans loved the many songs and dances in the film. The most famous scene shows actor Gene Kelly dancing and singing the title song of the film.

Gene Kelly in
Singin' in the Rain

Before Technicolor, some directors added color to their movies by hand-coloring every frame. That process was used as early as the 1890s. It was time-consuming but beautiful.

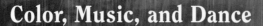

ballet scene from
An American in Paris

Another musical, *An American in Paris*, was also filmed in Technicolor. It has a special 17-minute ballet scene. It was one of the most complicated dance numbers ever produced.

Fans loved these musicals for their magic. Color was a big part of that magic. So were music and dance. They all worked together to tell stories.

The World Changes (Again)

A lot changed in the 1950s. The Great Depression and World War II were over. People had more money and more free time. They settled into comfortable home lives. Television sets became common. Old movies were sold to TV stations. People could watch them at home, and they did.

Filmmakers needed to find something that would bring people to the theater. TV sets at that time could only show black-and-white programs. Making movies in color was a way to give people something they could not get at home.

Technology in film also changed. Eastman Kodak found a way to make color film cheaper. The company made a type of film that could record in color. Filmmakers did not need a special camera with filters anymore. The new way was much less costly and time-consuming.

In 1955, the Technicolor company stopped making its special cameras. It still used its dyes to add color to film. It just used a different process.

Children watch TV in the 1950s.

People park at a drive-in theater to see a color movie in the 1950s.

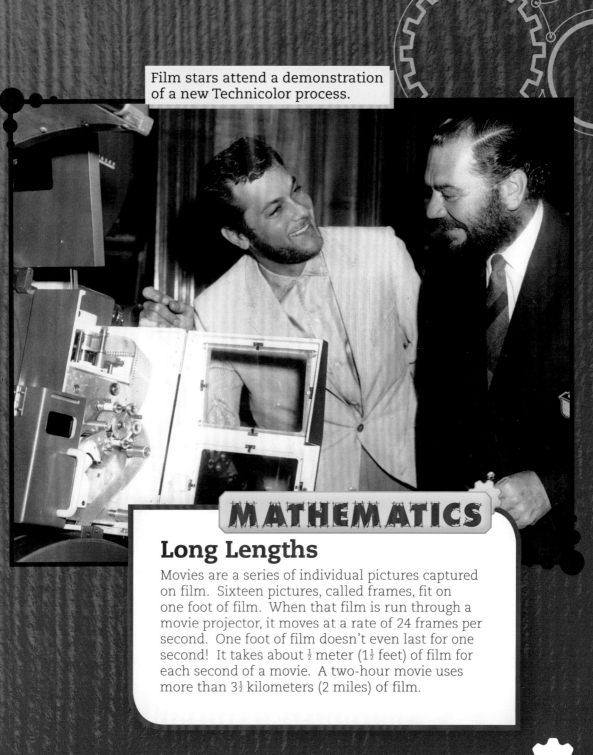

Film stars attend a demonstration of a new Technicolor process.

MATHEMATICS

Long Lengths

Movies are a series of individual pictures captured on film. Sixteen pictures, called frames, fit on one foot of film. When that film is run through a movie projector, it moves at a rate of 24 frames per second. One foot of film doesn't even last for one second! It takes about ½ meter (1½ feet) of film for each second of a movie. A two-hour movie uses more than 3½ kilometers (2 miles) of film.

After Technicolor Cameras

Fiddler on the Roof was released in Technicolor in 1971. By then, most filmmakers thought the process was too expensive and slow. There were much more efficient ways to make color films.

One of the last films printed by Technicolor was *The Godfather: Part II*. It came out in 1974. The next year, the company closed its dye plant in the United States.

a scene from *Fiddler on the Roof*

More Things Change…

Technology is still helping people change films. These changes both worry and please people. Many debates focus on how **computer graphics** are used in movies. Some people love them. Other people think they are the latest gimmick to hurt films.

model of Buzz Lightyear from *Toy Story*

In the 1990s, Disney released *Toy Story*, its first feature-length film that used computer **animation**. People worried that the movie would not be a hit because it looked so different from Disney movies of the past. Those people were quickly proven wrong. It was a huge hit.

An animator works on *Toy Story*.

Color Changes Everything

Technicolor made *The Wizard of Oz* magical. The vibrant colors of Oz told a story. The colors showed that Oz was a very different place from Dorothy's home in Kansas. Moviegoers loved the magic of the colors.

Many people worked hard to improve Technicolor over the years. They were a lot like the characters in *The Wizard of Oz*. They used their brains like the Scarecrow. They came up with different ways to make the process better. Like the Tin Man, they had heart. They did not give up when things did not work out. And, like the Cowardly Lion, they needed courage to do things that had never been done before.

At first, people didn't think color movies would last. But people liked watching movies in color. Filmmakers learned how to use color to help tell stories. It made movies better. People expect movies to be in color today. It is no longer fancy or new. There is no single person to thank for this. It was a combination of efforts. But without Technicolor, movies would look very different today.

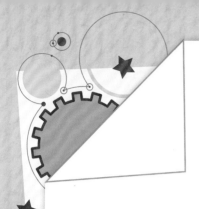

STEAM CHALLENGE

Define the Problem

Pretend you are on the audio-visual crew for your school's big play. During dress rehearsal, you notice that the color changer on your spotlight is broken and is only producing white light. You need to be able to produce different-colored lights for the night's performance. Your task is to create a filter that can show light in red, orange, yellow, green, blue, and purple.

 Constraints: Your filter must be made from items that are commonly found within a school or can be purchased at a common store.

 Criteria: Your filters must be able to switch between colors quickly. The more colors you can create, the better.

Research and Brainstorm

What colors can be created by mixing primary colors? What materials will let light pass through (i.e., are transparent)? How do people see color?

Design and Build

Make a plan of how to create each color and what materials will be used. Gather and assemble materials. Make your filter(s).

Test and Improve

Use a flashlight with your filter to see which colors can be created. What range of colors can you make? Can you adjust the shades of the colors? Modify your design and try again.

Reflect and Share

Were there any colors you could not create? Why couldn't you create them? If you had more time, could you create a different solution? Would it be a better idea? Why or why not?

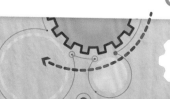

Glossary

animation—the process of making a series of pictures that look like they're moving because of small changes

ballet—a form of dance

bleak—not hopeful or encouraging

computer graphics—visual images that are created on computers

decades—periods of 10 years

dye—add color to material

filters—transparent materials, such as colored glass, that absorb light

gimmick—a trick used to attract attention

magenta—a bright, purplish-red color

muffle—to decrease the noise of something

technique—a way of doing something that uses special knowledge or skills

transfer—move from one place to another

vibrant—bright

Index

Do you want to learn about old films?
Here are some tips to get you started.

"The best way to learn about films is to watch as many as you can! Try to watch movies from different years. See how things have changed over the years. The future of film will probably combine new technology with classic stories."
—*Zarth Bertsch, Director of Theaters*

"Join a film club or an audio-visual club and learn how movies are made. Don't be afraid to try new techniques in film. After all, people thought Technicolor was a gimmick and it changed everything!"
—*Ryan Lintelman, Curator*